I've Been Meaning to Write

Ujjwala Singh

BookLeaf Publishing

India | USA | UK

Presentation by *BookLeaf Publishing*

Web: www.bookleafpub.com

E-mail: info@bookleafpub.com

ISBN:9789358735284

First edition 2023

DEDICATION

To Icarus's Sun

ACKNOWLEDGEMENT

I wouldn't have been able to publish this book without my support system. Mum, Dad, Karl, Yash, Keane - this is for you :)

Sit nomen domini benedictum

The Orchestral Prod

And so, the orchestra ensues
With no rests
No recuse
The crests, the troughs, the falls
Never seem to get me to the truth
Harmonious, oh yes
But disparagingly cruel

For if music is a journey
I am on a hunt
In the midst of a new found lament
I feel as though I'm on the cusp

And yet I cannot reach the end
The big percussion bang
Stuck here in this nightmare
Where the triangle's soft ding
Never rang

The signal never came
The instruments were meant to turn to props
Yet the symphony is going strong
The conductor never stops
My heart beats faster now
Picking up the pace

The cello strings, the baritone
They seem to me a warning sign Of something
deep below
The woodwinds hit their highest peak,
Slow down then crescendo
The final note comes out the pipe
In the end, I am alone.

Metamorphosis

Metamorphosis,
However beautiful,
Will always bring pain
But I promise
The stain-coloured wings we finally attain
Will be well worth the wait

Love is Found

5

Love is found
In hues of blue
All the shades I never even knew
Enter: You
The colour is no more symbolic of the ocean's
cruel truth
More so of a gleeful lover's youth

Love is found
In nothing more simply profound
Than a smile of mischief
And the warming sound
Of your steps moving towards me

Our call is paused
The world has stopped
Penny in the air
And the penny drops

As your smile meets mine

I'm here, I don't belong

Words & whispers,
Battered stares,
I have the grace of a Pitbull hurling down the
stairs

I am not here yet,
I do not belong,
And yet these hallowed halls,
Sing my favourite songs

I do not know yet when I will feel,
As though I am a part of this -
Concrete, real

So for now my respite,
Is found in empty chairs,
Three is a crowd
And one just isn't fair.

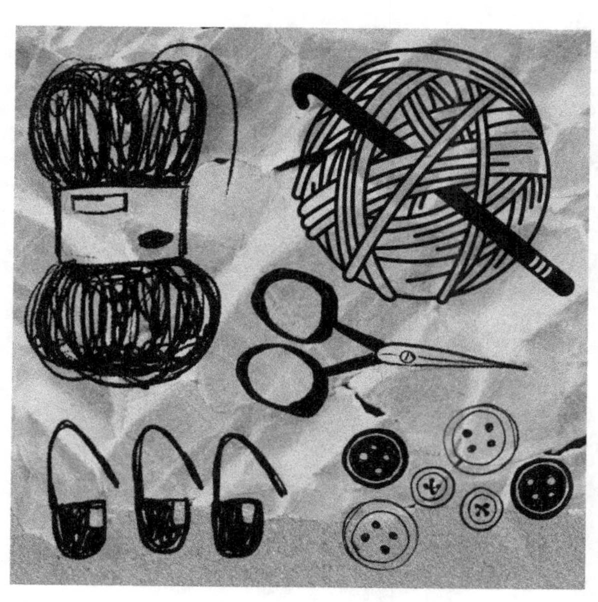

The Stocking Has Runs

9

A friend to all is a friend to none,
And as I sit here watching the red
Of the ebbing sun,
I realize, maybe our friendship was better
undone.

We were patchwork knitting, crotched fun,
Through the needles, I look down
And see
Our stocking always had runs

Repetitive Solace in the Ocean Blue

Was it my fault or yours?
Most likely mine,
I should've known that a running tide,
Could never truly stay immobile.

Alas!
I could've found solace in the crash of the
waves,
Some consolation in the ocean blue,
If only there wasn't so much semblance between
them
And you
Once thick as thieves, we now have no recuse.

In a fleeting moment you were all in,
The next MIA,
But over time your poker face has dismantled,
frayed,
I've learned to make mazes,
Out of the lines in your telling face.

I know now when the tide is preparing to retreat,
Never beg for it to stay.
In my repetitive solace,

I'm neither happy
Nor am I in dismay.

Rainwater Religion

The storm has arrived.

The soft corruption of rainwater fractions,

The sweet yearning, lingering within the cold
breeze's folds,

The sorrow entrapped in the dust upon the pane,

All begin their onerous ascent.

Journeying to be cradled by July's blanket greys,

For nature's sweet droplet offering,

Was born to push down on us.

Ease the angst heaving from our guilt riddled
bodies,

Release our beings,

From tumultuous flesh-coloured shells,

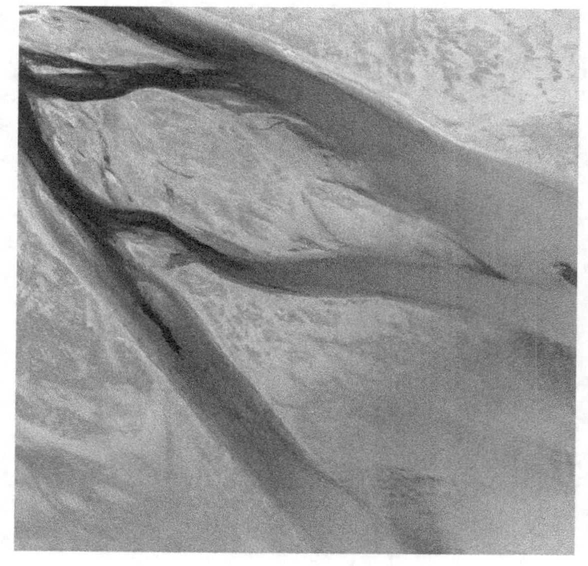

Because you see, the storm,

In all it's mighty terror,

Is a religion.

August's Concrete

17

My home teeters upon cotton candy whisps in
July.
Yet when August's leaves fall,
I plunge alongside their veins,
In a utopia for a fleeting moment,
In the devoid concrete the next.

Reciprocity

At age 8 I thought I knew love,
Knew what I'd do to keep it safe,
Nestled in the palms of my hands,
Where the feeling would remain forever chaste.
But times are destined to change,
And so are we,
I've learnt it is not safety that I now seek,
It's eager reciprocity.
For what is love without the ardent need,
To meet each other in the middle?
To remain mindlessly afloat, dangling between
the lines,
Amidst the battling desires,
Of two distinct minds,
I am peacefully surrendered and yet feverishly
alive.

My Walls

I wonder if my walls glimpsed me now,
What they would say
Would they miss the sickly warmth of the night?
The way my darkness clung to their chipped
paint?
The way it edged deeper in caution,
All the times there was nothing left to say.

Would they tell me I've run amok?
Command me to come home to the deathly
gloom?
Or would they see my new-found glow?
Fend me off if I ever tried to renew,
Our sordid friendship

Would they proclaim me a traitor?
A disgrace to who they once knew?
The girl who lived in the shadows,
Buried alive in a tomb
Of her own volition

Sealed the vault with her own bare hands,
However frail and thin,
Alas, they'd held the weight of all that passed,
And all that never came.

Perhaps they would understand?
Acknowledge that my past self was a shell?
An empty husk of the once loved poet,
Of the girl who fought back each time she fell.

I wonder if they'd even care.
To them, was I yet another passerby?
Could they ever truly trust
When they knew before we began, that I was
always condemned to say goodbye?

They keep me company on the nights of
desolation,
The walls that held me when I cried
Enclosed me in familial isolation,
When I hurt so much, I couldn't possibly stay
alive.

When the mornings spiralled into night,
And the nights never seemed to cease.
When my cloak shielded me from the warmth so
needed.
And my body was on a fleeting lease.

But I remind myself that the era is bygone,
That I have found myself anew
That every dark day has been enclosed in
rapture,
Every blackness replaced with clear blue

I remind myself I am safe
That I can finally close my eyes
I am safe to live, I am safe to love,
And to finally wish them goodnight

Rain in the Meadows

25

I wonder what the aged trees have seen,
Wrinkles on their barks, timber brown in
meadows full of green,
The fleeting quarrels of a road trip frenzy,
Or the exasperated sounds of runaway fiends?

Blistered souls with fettered blissful beams,
Untethered from earthly bounds and corporate
flings,
Where reach neither summer's gaze nor freshly
found spring
Rather than gloom, rain over here,
Is synonymous with 'free'

My Love

The Old Art of Love

27

Where touch is aplenty,
And boundaries remain few
My heart sits here in ache
For those stolen glances
Your eyes on me
Mine on you

Pockets of lovelorn letters,
A hideaway ruse,
Maybe two?
I lie in wait,
For fresh roses bought in my name,
Coloured in the same faint likeness as my
complexion's hue

Of Nights Spent Reading

Scents of pages,
All turned but one,
The moonlight shines
Where once perched, was the sun

The learned wisdom of blissful birds
Now turned to vacant incoherent chirps
And yet the story, my love, has just begun
The moon settles down, as should I
And up rises the sun

Warm Tea in Sunlight's Eyes

31

In the arms of my beloved
Under the sweet dew of sun
Wind's tides blow our linen curtains
And unanimously, all at once
We are in raptures
One stationery, one poised to run
In our endless game
Of cat, mouse and sun

Uncertain

I am in pastel raptures one moment
Navy blue and black the next
Leaving me unsure of my own preferences
Whether the cruel rains suit me better,
Or perhaps blistered sun adorns me best

I find solace in solitude at noon
And feel the most intensely forlorn by half past
five
All of these changes, I'm told
Are what will transform me,
Form the foundations of life

Of this, I am still uncertain.

Falling in Love

To love is to fall
And that's the way it should always be
It is not half-hearted content in a mundane tip
toeing
But a passionate, trusting, faithful leap

To love is to fall
And that's the way it has always been
It is not the caresses of a calm ocean breeze
But a tempest, thundering in the depths of an
incessant sea

To love is to fall
And this is how I wish it to stay
It is not the pleasant diffused beams of sunlight
after rain
But engulfing fiery rays
Of a merciless, panoptic beam
The kind that leaves its mark forever,
And that demands to be seen.

Lover's Tiff

I do not wish to walk in love and I do not wish
to run
Instead, I wish to sink until I am lost
Feeling everything all at once

I do not wait on silent smiles, echoing of gleeful
disregard
Instead, I wish for hearty laughter
That leave the neighbours begging for us to
depart

I do not look forward to conversations in sweet
nothings
Holding my peace forevermore
Instead, I hope for discomfort
Patient silences that strengthen rapport

I do not wish for lax compromise, a home filled
with an air of complacency
Instead, I wish for two raging beings
With so much yet so see
That they spend eternity in a lover's tiff
Under the happiness of the sun's warm gleam

Night at Sea

Is yellow my favourite colour?
How could it deign be
When in its absence the sky seems to love me
most
And my conscience only ever fills with
compassion
For witnesses to see

Perhaps a lack of colour would suit me best
Whatever fills a sailor's eyes
As he meets both his maker
And his despondent demise
Perhaps I am the tempest
Clinging to his dying body for respite

Stranded alone at sea
After the success of a vengeful feat
I become incapable of deciphering the simple
things
Was it him screaming in search of a saviour
Or me?

Y(earned)

Some days, friendship feels like a relic
As though it is always something passed
In the way wind feels on a summer's day
Enjoyed and then forgot

Nevertheless, I holdfast and yearn
Wish upon the evening star for the cool breeze to
return
I sit there and watch the clouds pass me by
In the hopes that maybe
Just maybe, friendship is something I can earn

For if it isn't?
I'm back to square one
Lack of empathy on my part, is not the problem
Its my overripe concern

My tendency to plead
With none other than myself
Afraid that if I open my eyes and truly feel
I'll be stranded, alone
Unattended in a raging sea
Of faces.

If I Were to Fall

And if I were to fall
I wish to be Icarus staring at his Sun
Thinking of nothing but how eternity without
your warmth
Would drive even the most content to
irrevocable ends

And if I were to fall
I wish to be Icarus, my deceitful laughter
soundless
For the chaos that multiplies with each meter
gravity augments
Allows for no other sense
But touch to be of use
Forlorn at the absence of your skin on mine

And if I were to fall
I wish to be Icarus
The sensation of my wings melting, seemingly
feeble
As my mind stills on the embers of the molten
fire stood in solitude behind your image
Entrusting each spark to keep you safe
forevermore
While I burn.

Puzzles

45

If we are a finished puzzle
Of all those we have ever loved
Each piece of us, a fragment of nostalgic
encumbrance
Of the traits that we have learned

Then perhaps, just perhaps,
There is beauty in the broken
In the frenzy
In the untameable

Perhaps, the inability to be seamless
And nevertheless hold strong
When held up against gravity's tests
Is a gift for which we should long.

www.ingramcontent.com/pod-product-compliance
Lightning Source LLC
LaVergne TN
LVHW051234200726
843510LV00011B/1571